MAKING MEN WHOLE

J. B. PHILLIPS

Making
Men Whole

WORD BOOKS, Publisher
Waco, Texas

MAKING MEN WHOLE by J. B. PHILLIPS

Copyright © 1973 by J. B. Phillips

First Word Paperback Printing — March 1973
Second Word Paperback Printing — July 1974

Printed in the United States of America

CONTENTS

FOREWORD   9

I.   GOD AND A WORLD DISINTEGRATED   15

II. THE ACTION AND THE AIM OF LOVE   37

III. THE WORK OF RECONCILIATION   59

IV. INNER RESOURCES FOR THE TASK   81

V.   COMPLETENESS IN CHRIST: IN TIME
     AND IN ETERNITY   105

PREFACE TO THIS EDITION

My publishers have kindly asked me to write a new Preface to this edition of *Making Men Whole*. At the same time I have been given the opportunity to make any alterations to the substance of the "addresses" which were given some years ago.

Plainly a great many things have happened since the early fifties. For example, the very first sputnik had not then been launched. Yet to-day we take for granted the man-made satellites, which have immeasurably improved man's means of communication. So quickly do we accept the development of mankind's technology, that we read with hardly any surprise that an estimated 600 million viewers saw the landing of the first man on the moon. Perhaps we need to remind ourselves that not many years ago few people possessed television sets, transitor radios were unknown, and very few people knew anything about such commonplace domestic possessions as tape-recorders and stereophonic record reproducers.

These are, of course, but a few random samples of modern technological advance; there are literally thousands more. Those that we understand, even partially, cannot but command a good deal of admiration for the human ingenuity and persistent effort involved. Yet, in a sense, this kind of advance only intensifies the problem of how to learn to live together in peace. Even more now than when I first wrote of the "great acceleration of God's 'one increasing purpose'" we are being forced to realise that we are all members of the vast family of God. No man, least of all a Christian, can be deaf and blind to the agonies of disease, starvation, poverty, violence, persecu-

tion and all the monstrous forces of pain and evil which
rack our fellow-men.

This is no time for a holy pietism which withdraws
from a dangerous world into the safety of a fixed and
immutable Church. Indeed it would appear to me that
God is, so to speak, violently shaking the existing Churches.
Cracks have appeared in the most monolithic institutions,
while traditional Christian modes of thought and work
have been radically challenged both from within and without the Church. Reforms, unthinkable only a few short
years ago, have taken place and many more are inevitable.
The urge for unity among all Christian people is strong
and growing, despite the prejudices, fears and last-ditch
conservatism of some in all Churches.

It would, of course, be easy to "write off" this desire
for unity as a mere panic-measure for survival, no more
than a call to close the ranks against an increasingly
hostile world. I am sure that those who know Christians
(as against merely nominal Church-supporters) could not
agree. Those who have travelled the Christian world
extensively are forcibly struck by the evidence of something,
above the merely human, which is not only revitalising
long-dead Churches but relentlessly pressing them to seek
unity with all who hold the Christian faith in heart and
mind. For myself I cannot see this as anything less than
the pressure of the Spirit of the living God.

Meanwhile a growing number, not entirely in agreement
among themselves nor much organised, have quite
deliberately denounced the Church as irrelevant to the
modern world, and declared unequivocally that "God is
dead". Some of them, I feel myself, are unconscious
Christians, particularly those who give themselves to
the care and service of others. It would be, to my mind,
nothing short of blasphemous to deny that such dedicated

men and women are, however unconsciously, co-operating with the Will of God. But the main body of scientific humanists see neither the need for, nor the point of, the Christian God.

I believe the atheistic-humanist is tragically and in a sense suicidally wrong. By refusing to accept any dimension of " the spirit " and by rejecting any idea of that dimension which, for want of a better word, we call " eternity," he is working in a self-made cul-de-sac. I see no reason to change the exposure of the position (printed below on pages 124-125) which I made a few years ago, and I have never had a satisfactory reply to it from any intelligent humanist. By denying the reality of " eternity " we both diminish man's stature as a son of God and reduce his ultimate hope to vanishing point. Without God, with His limitless resources in dimensions yet unknown to us, our most frantic humane work is as pitiable and absurd as that of a housewife who insists on laying new carpets and hanging fresh curtains while her house is on fire.

We must be honest, and we must admit that the Church has, over the centuries, been often terribly and horribly to blame. In every century and in every country where there have been Christians, there have been many shining and honourable exceptions. But taking a broad view of her history we cannot in all honesty deny that the currently held " image " of herself is to a large extent her own fault. She has cared, but not deeply enough; she has served, but without sufficient humility. She has, for the most part, been faithful in the worship of Almighty God, but she has been habitually unwilling to follow the example of His Son. She has clung to power, privilege, wealth and safety, where He, Jesus, God's Christ, cared for none of these things. He gave *Himself*, and His followers can expect no more privilege or protection than their Master.

But the Christian Church is becoming more and more aware of this, and I am not at all sure that it isn't the compassionate humanist (who has no use for Church or God) who has not made her look long and hard at her words and actions, and indeed at her whole part in God's agonising task in reconciling human beings both to Himself and to one another.

Thus after much thought and careful re-reading I have left the following chapters largely unchanged. For I believe with all my heart that it is only those who are in touch with the living God who can do any truly effective and lasting good in our anxious, needy and tortured world.

I should not like to be misunderstood here. It is quite unrealistic to pretend that we live in the first century A.D., and it is equally foolish to imagine that any modern problem can be solved by quoting verses of the New Testament, however inspired they may be. But it can do us nothing but good to restudy the character of the Man who was also God, to see how He dared to follow the "awful, patient" ways of His Father (Who is also ours). We can also study how the tiny but intrepid band of early Christians attempted to do God's Will in a cruel, dark, and bitterly hostile world. And when we do these things we may remind ourselves, for our encouragement and our hope, that the Master promised that His Spirit would lead us into all truth; a promise that should surely keep us flexible and open-minded. Above all, He guaranteed that He would be with us always, to the end of time —and beyond it.

J. B. PHILLIPS

Golden Cap,
Gannets Park,
Swanage, Dorset.
1969

FOREWORD

THE following five chapters represent the substance of the Bible Readings which I was asked to give during the first week of the Church Missionary Society's Summer School at Bangor in 1952. The title, *Making Men Whole*, represents the dominant thought of our prayer and study together. As an introduction to the appearance of these Bible Readings in book form, I would underline the following points which seem to me basic to our theme:

1. Many Christians suffer to-day, more perhaps than in any preceding age, from a sense that the world is out of control. The impact of world tensions and problems is often so great that Christians, because they see and feel and care more than non-Christians, frequently become over-anxious and exaggerate their own responsibilities. We all need to be reminded that God is by no means baffled or bewildered by mankind's muddles and follies. We all need to remember that our strength lies in quietness and confidence, not in frantic challenges and hysterical efforts. The world remains primarily God's responsibility,

and the best we can do is to find out our own part in His vast purpose and make sure that we are fulfilling that to the limit of our ability.

2. Most Christians are affected far more than they know by the standards and methods of the surrounding world. In these days when power and size and speed are almost universally admired, it seems to me particularly important to study afresh the " weakness," the " smallness of entry " and the " slowness " of God as He began His vast work of reconstucting His disordered world. We are all tempted to take short cuts, to work for quick results and to evade painful sacrifice. It is therefore essential that we should look again at love incarnate in a human being, to see God Himself at work within the limitations of human personality, and to base our methods on what we see Him do.

3. The writers of the New Testament Epistles never regarded the Christian religion as an " ethic," still less a performance. To them it was an invasion of their own lives by the living Spirit of God; their response in repentance and faith provided the means by which the divine could penetrate the merely human. They lived lives of super-human quality because they believed quite

simply that Christ Himself was alive within them.

For some reason or other we seem to regard this belief as somewhat presumptuous, and much of our present-day Christianity is a rather gauche performance designed to please an external God. The real presumption, indeed the impertinence, of our modern attitude is that we do not really accept God's full generosity; we do not really believe that Christ is alive and operative in every true disciple.

4. The pressure of world events, as well as of the gentle leading of the Spirit of God Himself, is making it plain to the dimmest human intelligence that men must learn to live together as one family or perish from the earth altogether. Thus I believe that we can say, without unduly dramatising ourselves, that we live in a time of great acceleration of God's " one increasing purpose." In Christ alone is there integration for the individual, for the Churches, and for the whole scattered human family. The purpose itself, in its scope and depth, is becoming clearer, and the most important issue confronting any one of us is the question: " Am *I* co-operating with the purpose, or not? "

5. If we are to have a " whole " view of life

and its purpose, it is very necessary for us to recover the sense that this human life of ours is lived *sub specie æternitatis*. In our modern pre-occupation with Christian social justice and the relevance of the Christian faith to all human problems, we tend to forget the heaven to which we are bound. Unless we have this essential background we are left with too many unsolved problems and too many flagrant injustices for us to believe confidently in the love of God. Quite apart from the question of rewards, punishments and compensations, we do not allow God sufficient " elbow-room " in this restricted sphere for the final working out of His awful patient purpose. We must recover the wonder and glory of the calling wherewith we are called.

Nothing that I have written is new; all of it is based on the Scripture passages which are printed at the head of each chapter. But we need constantly to be reminded of those eternal truths by which alone we can face this life with courage, hope and good humour.

J. B. PHILLIPS

St. John's Vicarage,
Redhill, Surrey,
August, 1952

I.

God and a World Disintegrated

New Testament passages which should be studied in connection with the following chapters are :

ST. JOHN X.   VERSES 1 TO 16

Then Jesus said, " Believe Me when I tell you that anyone who enters into the sheepfold by any other way than the door is a thief and a rogue. It is the shepherd of the flock who goes in by the door. It is to him the door-keeper opens the door and it is his voice that the sheep recognise. He calls his own sheep by name and leads them out of the fold and when he has driven all his own flock outside, he goes in front of them himself, and the sheep follow him because they know his voice. They will never follow a stranger—indeed, they will run away from him, for they do not recognise strange voices."

Jesus gave them this illustration but they did not grasp the point of what He was saying to them. So Jesus said to them once more, " I do assure you that I Myself am the ' door ' for the sheep. All who have gone before Me are like thieves and rogues but the sheep did not listen to them. I am the ' door.' If a man goes in through Me, he will be safe and sound ; he can come in and out and find his food. The thief comes with the sole intention of stealing and killing and destroying, but I came to bring them life, and far more life than before. I am the good shepherd. The good shepherd gives his life for the sake of his sheep. But the hired man, who is not the shepherd, and does not own the sheep, sees the wolf coming, deserts the sheep and runs away. And the wolf will attack the flock and send them flying. The hired man runs away because he is only a hired man and has no interest in the sheep. I am the good shepherd, and I know those that are Mine and My sheep know Me, just as the Father knows Me and I know the Father. And I am giving My life for the sake of the sheep.

"And I have other sheep who do not belong to this fold. These also I must lead, and they will hear My voice. So there will be one flock and one Shepherd."

EPHESIANS II. VERSES 4 TO 18

But even though we were dead in our sins God was so rich in mercy that He gave us the very life of Christ (for it is, remember, by grace and not by achievement that you are saved), and has lifted us right out of the old life to take our place with Him in Christ in the heavens. Thus He shows for all time the tremendous generosity of the grace and kindness He has expressed towards us in Christ Jesus. It was nothing you could or did achieve— it was God's gift to you. No one can pride himself that he earned the love of God. The fact is that what we are we owe to the Hand of God upon us. We are born afresh in Christ, and born to do those good deeds which God planned for us to do.

Do not lose sight of the fact that you were born "Gentiles," known by those whose bodies were circumcised as "the Uncircumcised." You were without Christ, you were utter strangers to God's chosen community, the Jews, and you had no knowledge of, or right to, the promised Agreements. You had nothing to look forward to and no God to Whom you could turn. But now, through the blood of Christ, you who were once outside the pale are with us inside the circle of God's love and purpose. For Christ is our living Peace. He has made a unity of the conflicting elements of Jew and Gentile by breaking down the barrier which lay between us. By His sacrifice He removed the hostility of the Law, with all its commandments and rules, and made in Himself out of the two, Jew and Gentile, One New Man, thus producing peace. For He reconciled both to God by the sacrifice of one Body on the Cross, and by this act made utterly irrelevant the antagonism between them. Then He came and told both you who were far from God and us who were near that the war was over. And it is through Him that both of us now can approach the Father in the one Spirit.

I

GOD AND A WORLD DISINTEGRATED

WE FACE to-day a world torn and divided. So
widespread is the distress of nations, so complex
the problems which face every thinking Christian,
that I think we may be forgiven if our hearts
sometimes fail us. There is no need to elaborate
here the problems and distresses which confront
us on every hand. Probably we are only too well
aware of them. But for our comfort we may
fairly remind ourselves that the world-wide
tensions and sufferings only seem to us to be
more overwhelming than they did to our forefathers because we are much better informed
about them through modern means of news-
transmission than they could ever be. To-day,
with vastly improved communications of all
kinds, we are aware of what is happening in
distant places, whereas our forefathers could live
much more parochially and usually with little
sense of world problems.

This difference is not, of course, entirely a

matter of news-communication, for during the
last century the nations have become infinitely
more inter-dependent than ever before in the
history of the world. To be isolationist or
parochial has become not only un-Christian but
impossible. What happens in China, or Africa,
or the United States can no longer be of merely
academic interest to us; it can affect profoundly
our actual lives. A hundred years ago or less, it
would have been fantastic to suggest that a
struggle in far-off Korea, for example, could
have the faintest bearing on the private life of an
ordinary Englishman, even if he knew about it.
To-day we are so inter-related that the problems
of distant countries affect not merely our minds
and hearts but our very mode of living, whether
we like it or not. In days gone by there could
be famines, plagues, bitter wars, earthquakes and
disasters, happening maybe on a vast scale in a
far-away continent, and we should have known
nothing of them. But to-day we hear of these
things, we read of them, we see pictures of
them on the news-reels, and even the least
sensitive can hardly say: "This is no concern
of mine."

To put it another way, the vast achievements
of science through improved travelling and

communications have borne in upon the sensitive soul, and more slowly upon the insensitive, the fact that we are, however divided, "all in it together." There has never been a time in the history of the world when men have thought and calculated in global terms as to-day they must. And there is, of course, no arresting of this progress, no preventing of the awakening from sleep of continent and race. We as Christians are probably more sensitive than anyone else to the fact that for the first time in the history of the human race men have got to learn to live together as a family. And because we know how deep-rooted are human sins and frailties, we are more aware than others of how difficult this problem must inevitably be.

We need not, however, be overwhelmed by the prospect before us, for two reasons. First because this is God's world, and although we may be bewildered by the speed at which the world is awakening before our eyes, we can be quite sure that there is no bewilderment in the mind of God. This is His world and since He knows the end from the beginning, we can at all times be confident that at any given moment in the world's history there is, for those who

will listen to His voice, a right way of meeting
the complexities of the contemporary situation,
even though that right way cannot in the nature
of things achieve in a single generation the
perfect will of God.

Then again, we need constantly to remind
ourselves that no single one of us and no single
group of us is required to carry more responsibility than we can bear. We may well feel battered,
bruised and bewildered by the continual assault
of news, of problems put before us, of challenges
thrown down to us. But each man has his proper
work to do and no single one of us is required
to do more than the will of God for him. The
famous words, " In His will is our peace," are
perfectly true here as in other contexts. If we
attempt to do more than His will, if we allow
ourselves to be stampeded into responsibilities
beyond our powers by the vastness of the
problems around us, we lose our peace. We need,
as St. Paul told the Thessalonians, " to study to
be quiet and to do our own business " (1 Thessalonians iv. 11 *A.V.*). In doing our part of
God's will we shall find peace, but in attempting
more than our part we shall find only anxiety
and frustration.

This truth needs to be thought out by all who

share a common interest in the world-wide work of the Church. We can so easily become tense and over-anxious just because we are sensitive to the world's need, and thereby fail effectually to do that small part of the task which God has allotted to us. Because of the magnitude of the problems which press upon us we may even seek to evade such frightening responsibilities. But if we will keep in mind the fact that the ultimate responsibility belongs to God and be willing to accept, not the whole of the world's burden but that part which God has marked out for us to carry, we shall be able to accept His call to maintain our peace and do our work effectually.

It is necessary to point out that our responsibility is a relative one only, for as we think of the world-wide disintegration of the human family the prospect before us could easily fill us with alarm and despondency, if we were not sure first of the absolute sovereignty of God who (I speak reverently) knows what He is doing in conducting this enormous experiment that we call life. Secondly, though we often think in terms of world issues, the majority of us are not called to be world leaders or anything like it, but sensible and faithful servants of the One whose purpose it is to unite the scattered races under one Shepherd.

In St. John x. our Lord contrasts Himself as the *Good* Shepherd in whose care the sheep find food and security, with the thieves and robbers who came before Him. I have often wondered whom He had in mind, for the words as they stand, " All who have gone before Me are like thieves and rogues " (St. John x. 8) sound rather harsh. It is probable that in the contemporary situation Christ had in mind leaders of men, political, national and even religious, who really, in the long run, destroyed or stole for their own ends the souls of men. There are many " thieves and rogues " in the situation to-day who are similarly exploiting and destroying personality. We think of the soul-destroying aims and methods of Communism; of false religions which ask so much of men and in the end give them nothing. There are those who deliberately destroy the souls of men by the sale of harmful drugs, the marketing of sex and its manifold perversions, and the exploitation of the obscene through pornography. There are those who deliberately inflame religious or racial prejudice and destroy the very possibility of understanding and integration. We think of the blight of materialism which by flattering a man's importance in this life deprives him of his destiny as a son of God. We think of the reckless pursuit of pleasure which meets man's love of beauty and happiness with the tawdry and the meretricious.

Within a man's own personality there is no lack of " thieves and rogues." There is his driving ambition which without the influence of Christ becomes, sooner or later, a destructive tyrant; there is his pride which insulates him from his neighbour and sows enmity between his group and another. Above all, there is his fear, rooted of course in pride and self-love, which drives out the milk of human kindness and which in its extreme forms makes him behave far worse than the animal creation. We have to face the fact that in the individual man as well as in society there have always been these disintegrating factors, the " thieves and rogues " who, though often unseen, are quietly at work. Yet wherever He is given the chance, there is the integrating factor, the Good Shepherd Himself, seeking to make men whole, seeking to integrate both human personality and the whole human family.

This problem of making men whole, of integrating them as persons and unifying them in a

community, is much more difficult than some
idealists might suppose. The "thieves and
rogues," the disintegrating forces, have had a
very long innings. They are deeply entrenched,
their cumulative infection is overwhelming, and
they are by no means always recognised for what
they are. It is quite literally a superhuman task
to plunge into the welter of centuries of disintegration and begin to make men whole.

At the risk of repetition it must be emphasised
that what we are beginning to envisage nowadays
is a much larger-scale and more widespread integration than our forefathers as a general rule imagined. The salvation of an individual soul is indeed
important, but we are beginning to see that the
work of the Good Shepherd goes deeper and
wider than we ever supposed. It is true that His
plan considers the importance of the single
"sheep"; under the Good Shepherd the one sheep
can be saved and "come in and out and find his
food" (St. John x. 9). But the plan is far greater
than that. There are the "other sheep" (St. John x.
16) at present astray, who must also be brought into the fold. It is not only the so-called contemporary pressures which make us feel that we are "all in
this together"; to those who are sensitive to the
breath of the Spirit, it is surely God Himself who

is widening our horizons, mentally and spiritually, and making us feel and see the breath-taking compass of His integrating purpose.

Nothing less than a world-wide principle of wholeness, a world-loving and world-loved King and Shepherd will suffice for our modern need. In the past, so long as men were broken up into more or less self-contained units, it was not altogether impossible to secure an integration which was local and to some extent superficial. The rules and customs of a tribe, for example, the unquestioned but purely parochial authority of their king, priest or leader produced such a limited "wholeness." In our own country, there sometimes existed in a village, for example, such a circumscribed integration. And no doubt in many countries a similar local harmony was often achieved. But the need to-day, as is obvious to anyone with eyes to see, is for something at once more penetrating and more far-reaching than that limited conception. Indeed, on examination we find that the apparent wholeness of little communities was due at least in part to fear of other communities; and the very loyalty which preserved the local cohesion would effectually prevent co-operation with similar communities. In our Lord's day, for example, there was a certain

cohesive loyalty about the Jews which produced
in both personality and community some magnificent results. Yet it was exclusive "for Jews have
nothing to do with Samaritans" (St. John iv. 9),
and they regarded the Gentiles with, at the best,
a tolerant contempt. We hardly realise the ex-
plosive quality of St. Paul's inspiration when,
under the influence of the new integrating force,
he declared that in Christ "gone is the distinction
between Jew and Greek, slave and free man,
male and female" (Galatians iii. 28).

It may be a little presumptuous and it may be
a little premature, but it seems to me that in this
twentieth century, with the whole inhabited
world awakening and opening up before our
eyes, we have the chance for the first time to see
the vastness of God's integrating plan. The
apparent insignificance of its beginning is breath-
taking. For if we strip away for a moment the
romance and decoration of the Christmas story,
we stand aghast at the awe-inspiring humility of
God's beginning of His task of integration. The
things which look romantic on a Christmas card
or which sound pretty by association with
delightful carols, were in fact most devastatingly
humble. For a pregnant woman to hunt desperately for a room when her time drew near

would hardly be our choice for God's entry into the world on human terms! And yet so it was. That is how He came, right in at the human level: The Word of wholeness was born into a world of misery and strife, of suffering and sin.

It is the temptation not only of politicians and law-makers, but of religious people as well, to think that people can be made whole and that they can be induced to live together in harmony, by fiats of authority. Yet when God began His work of personal rescue, there was no trump from heaven, there were no supporting armies of angels. In the Man who was God in human form, God focused and scaled down to meet our human need, we find One " gentle and humble in heart," who allowed the thieves and rogues of humanity to close in upon Him and kill Him. He had, He has, a frightening patience; frightening, that is, to us who have so little faith and have such a lust for quick results. But the work of making men whole was begun.

Although the coming of the integrating principle into a dark, perplexed and infected world began, so to speak, on the ground level, can we not begin to see that this is, without qualification, the only way in which God, or for that matter any power whatsoever, could restore wholeness to mankind? Every effort to impose wholeness by regulation from above must fail, partly because it is for ever external to human nature itself; partly because it neither excites the love nor provides the power to overcome human spiritual poverty. St. Paul was right when he said the law " was weak " (Romans viii. 3 A.V.). When it attempted to change human nature it was not weak in one sense, in that it represented the eternal principles of human conduct. But it was completely powerless in practice because of its utter incapacity to change man's nature from within.

In Ephesians ii. St. Paul speaks with confidence having observed the result of God's method through Christ. Into human life and at the human level, He, so to speak, inserts His own life with its immeasurable potentialities for converting, redeeming, reconciling and bringing into harmony. From the world's point of view, this low-level approach was and still is a ridiculously weak and impracticable way of tackling the deep-rooted problems of human nature. Yet it has worked, not invariably and not without failure, but with a result so impressive that even a hostile world cannot disregard it. New powers, new qualities, a new spirit came to birth and began at once to work upon even the most unpromising material to produce whole men, and of humanity a Whole Man. The process has continued ever since, and though our faith is small and our experience limited, we have all seen things happen which were never possible in a pagan world. With this astonishing apparent weakness God is at work with a kind of loving relentlessness to make " in Himself . . . One New Man, thus producing peace " (Ephesians ii. 15).

There then are the two contrasting energies at work, marring or making for wholeness in the lives of men: on the one hand the big noisy, apparently unconquerable passions of the world, which are the " thieves and rogues " of man's true nature; and on the other, the quiet, gentle, but immensely powerful work of the Good Shepherd.

But there is something vital to add, in terms of man's response. The Church began with the super-naturally inspired insight of Peter who cried: " You are Christ, the Son of the living God " (St. Matthew xvi. 16). Up to that moment, if we may look at things reverently from Christ's point of view, there had been swirling tides

of emotion among the people whom He met.
Popular enthusiasm ran high; He was the great
Healer, He was the wonderful Teacher, He
was a reincarnation of one of the prophets of
old. But all this was an unreliable floating tide
of opinion. Then came Peter's inspired remark,
and at once our Lord (God walking the earth as
a human being), seized upon the solidity of real
faith. " You are Peter the rock! " He cried out,
in delight I think, " And it is upon this rock that
I am going to found my Church " (St. Matthew
xvi. 18). To Christ's matchless insight here was
the beginning of this world-wide fellowship of
men and women of all races. Here was the tiny
beginning of the society which would transcend
all barriers of colour, class and custom, yes, and
even time and space as well. For Peter, in a
moment of true faith, had seen who Christ really
was.

To see and to recognise who Jesus Christ
really was and is, makes the whole vast work of
rescue possible. Prophets, poets, idealists, all
have their message to give, but until someone
sees that God Himself has penetrated into human
life at man's own level, there can be no real
beginning to the work of making men whole.
Without this recognition, there is no certainty,

only a feeling. Without this recognition, there
is no ultimate certainty, only a hopeful idealism.
Without this certainty, there is no observable
purpose in all the ills and accidents, the injustices
and the bitter disappointments in this transitory
part of existence that we call life. But once this
recognition has come to birth, the certainty is
there, the guarantee is there, the power is there,
the authority, the plan and the purpose are all
there, and the building can begin. No wonder
Christ said of Peter's outburst of faith, " on *this*
rock I am going to found my Church."

It is most noteworthy that this certainty runs
right through the New Testament. It is as though
men were using then a faculty which to-day is
largely atrophied, the faculty of faith. They were
not so much holding on desperately despite the
evidence of a hostile world—their faith amounted
to knowledge. They knew: they knew God;
they knew the purpose and plan of God; they
knew the power of God. And although from
our modern point of view their outlook was
restricted, in many ways they could see farther
than we, and by the inspiration of the Spirit of
God they gained more than a glimpse of the
majestic sweep of God's vast purpose. Before
we can move in the matter, before we can be

made whole ourselves or take an active, telling part in the work of making men whole, we have to recapture that certainty. It is true that we are surrounded on all sides by uncertainty, but so were they. It is true that we are confronted by all kinds of evil, by a world at sixes and sevens with itself, but so were they. We may be sure that God has not changed, nor has His purpose been altered by the centuries. I confess I can see no valid reason why we should not use that faculty for " putting our full confidence in the things we hope for . . . being certain of things we cannot see " (Hebrews xi. 1). This is not a modern problem, though modern pressures have almost persuaded us that it is. It would be a great thing if God could show each one of us that we still have that faculty of faith, puny and undeveloped though it may be, and teach us how greatly He could work if we could cease from our anxieties and our preoccupations and reach out to contact the unseen but thoroughly dependable realities.

We need then first of all to recapture Christian certainty which is not a superior form of wishful thinking, but a regrasping of the purpose and plan of God by a faculty which, though long disused, is implanted in every child of God.

II.

The Action and the Aim of Love

New Testament passage which should be studied in connection with the following chapter is :

I JOHN IV. VERSES 7 TO THE END

To you whom I love I say, let us go on loving one another, for love comes from God. Every man who truly loves is God's son and has some knowledge of Him But the man who does not love cannot know Him at all, for God is love.

To us, the greatest demonstration of God's love for us has been His sending His only Son into the world to give us Life through Him. We see real love, not in the fact that we loved God, but that He loved us and sent His Son to make personal atonement for our sins. If God loved us as much as that, surely we, in our turn, should love each other !

It is true that no human being has ever had a direct vision of God. Yet if we love each other God does actually live within us, and His love grows in us towards perfection. And, as I wrote above, the guarantee of our living in Him and His living in us is the share of His own Spirit which He gives us.

II

THE ACTION AND THE AIM OF LOVE

St. Paul once said that " belief can only come
by hearing the message, and the message is the
word of Christ " (Romans x. 17), and that is a
most important statement. For it implies that
we have within us not merely the power for
holding on to a set of ideas which we believe to
be good, but also the faculty for grasping and
comprehending the truth of God. To many
somewhat depressed Christians to-day there
comes at times the feeling that they are clinging
to an interpretation of life which they believe to
be the truth, but which the world around regards
as merely one of many interpretations. This is
an unnecessarily depressed attitude, for the
Christian is by faith reaching out and touching
the real world. He is putting his full confidence
" in the things we hope for "; he is " certain
of things we cannot see " (Hebrews xi. 1). For
the word of God which stimulates and sustains
faith is eternal truth breaking through into this

temporary world, so that the certainty of the early Christians which we may regard with a certain wistfulness means, not that they were necessarily men of exceptional spiritual calibre, but simply that they recognised the word of God as being quite literally the message, plan and command of God Himself. It was a faith more rock-like than any human certainty which gave their lives their astonishing quality.

To-day we need to purge ourselves of any lingering thoughts that the Christian Gospel (and the spreading of that Gospel) is simply a good idea to be held tenaciously rather as men will hold on to a political theory. It is infinitely more than this; we hold in our hands " the very word of life " (Philippians ii. 16). We share, incredible as it may seem, part of the plan of God Himself; to some extent we are even in His confidence, for we know something of His methods and the vast scope of His purpose.

In the midst then of human conflicts, tensions and sufferings, there comes to those who believe the word of God far more than an inkling of what God is attempting. Once we accept Jesus Christ as the planned focusing of God in history, our faith becomes a certainty and we know, not indeed the whole of God, but what sort of a

Person God is, what kind of plan He is attempting to work out, and what sort of people we ought to be in co-operating with that purpose. We learn how *we* may be made whole; we learn along which lines the world may be made whole; and to us is given something far more than the ability to stand in this faith. " We win," as St. Paul said, " an overwhelming victory through Him Who has proved His love for us " (Romans viii. 37). Ours is no bare victory against the world, the flesh and the devil, won by the skin of our teeth. It is far more; God gives us the power and the love to overflow into the world about us.

Let us remind ourselves then of the character of God, the methods of God, and the resources of God. Our authority for these reminders is the New Testament, which is not only a unique collection of historical documents containing the record of the actual physical life of God when He became man, but of the actual demonstrable results which followed when men, by His Spirit, lived out His way of life. The New Testament is uniquely inspired because through these human, unself-conscious documents there comes again and again the authentic word of God—

truths breaking through like shafts of light from the real eternal world into the darkness of this temporary one.

The beginning of our certainty, the conviction that lies behind the task of making men and nations whole, lies in three simple words written by St. John, namely : " God is love " (1 John iv. 8 and 16).   I sometimes wish we could appreciate this, the primal fact of all existence, with fresh and unprejudiced minds, for there are several difficulties which stand in the way of our accepting this statement at its face value—which is surely what we should do.

First, in modern parlance the word "love" has become demoted and indeed debased to mean all sorts of things. A man can have a love for Beethoven's String Quartets and a love for chocolates with hard centres ; he can love driving an open car at high speed ; but when he wants to express what he feels for the One who has touched the deepest roots of his being and wants, as all lovers do, to declare himself, he can only use the same word ! Whether it is due to paucity of language or mere carelessness, we find the same word used for a romantic but passing affection as for a lifetime's devotion and service. Yet the image of God is by no means altogether

defaced in mankind, and a great many people,
though they use the word carelessly or even
sentimentally, have some idea of what love really
means. Their deepest experiences are all strongly
connected with love and even the careless and the
superficial quite frequently have a wistful
admiration for genuine love.

The second difficulty is that men have been
afraid to proclaim the astonishing vulnerability
of the love of God. Its generosity is indeed awe-
inspiring, but in putting our message before
men we have no right so to qualify the love of
God, so to surround it with caveats and provisos,
that it ceases to be love at all in the commonly
accepted meaning of the term. Jesus once
declared that God is " good to the ungrateful
and the wicked " (St. Luke vi. 35), and I remember preaching a sermon on this text to a horrified
and even astounded congregation who simply
refused to believe (so I gathered afterwards) in
this astounding liberality of God. That God
should be in a state of constant fury with the
wicked seemed to them only right and proper,
but that God should be kind towards those who
were defying or disobeying His laws seemed to
them a monstrous injustice. Yet I was but
quoting the Son of God Himself, and I would

only comment here that the terrifying risks that God takes are part of His nature. We do not need to explain or modify His unremitting love towards mankind; all we know is that it is both constant, impartial and unearned.

Then again we have the distressing phenomenon exhibited by some Christians of love in inverted commas! " Let us have no imitation Christian love," wrote St. Paul (Romans xii. 9), and I sometimes wonder whether he had this artificial love in mind. I think I know how it comes about. Christians are commanded to love, and unless they allow their own hearts to be both humbled and purged by the vast love of God, they are likely to exhibit a purely superficial attitude of love towards those who are not Christians, or even towards Christians who are not of their school of thought. They cannot really bear to be vulnerable, as love always must be; to be imposed upon, humiliated or ridiculed, as love often may be. Yet not only do they impoverish their own lives; they are at least partly responsible for the impression which many people have that Christian love is somehow not quite genuine, and that when Christians declare that God is love, they mean that behind a smiling providence He hides a frowning face!

Somehow Christians must recapture on a grand

scale this basic certainty that God *is* love. Unless
they do, unless they feel it and know it and show
it and live it, it is unlikely that the surrounding
world, burdened by the apparent contradictions
and all the ills and accidents of this mortal life,
will ever grasp the fundamental fact of all creation.

If we were to study, without preconceived
ideas, the life of Christ as recorded in the Gospels;
if with fresh minds we could consider that life
fairly and squarely, I am certain that we should
be very surprised. So much is read back into the
story, so much majesty and even solemnity is
added by the matchless beauty of the Authorised
Version, that I doubt whether many of us have
had an unencumbered and unprejudiced view of
incarnate love. Yet, I believe we ought to try,
even if it means a stern effort of will and the
free exercise of our God-given imagination.

Let me mention three salient points among
many which baffled and bothered the early
disciples, and which baffle and bother us—until
we see that God really did enter unarmed at our
own level, and that He is really love, and not
someone pretending to be love, with a big stick
within easy reach!

(1) His attitude towards "sinners." To the
religious people of His day it was a scandalous

thing that Jesus, unlike the prophets of old, made no denunciation of those who were called sinners ; and we too may find it, if not scandalous, at least surprising. Jesus almost never called men sinners, except in the case of the entrenched self-righteous, whom we will consider in a moment. Perhaps I make this point clearer if, speaking for myself, I say that a high-pressure evangelist, whose technique depended on arousing and fostering a sense of guilt, would find himself woefully short of ammunition if he were only allowed to use as his texts the recorded words of Christ. With the common run of ordinary sinners, Jesus appears to have used the method of simple love. The sense of guilt, it would appear, might well take care of itself ; so far as we can judge He did not attempt to arouse it. Consequently, we find Matthew, loved and appreciated as a man perhaps for the first time for many years, giving up a profitable racket and following One who called him in love. We find Zaccheus, whose keen business instincts had shut him off from love and friendship, instantly melting into astonishing generosity when love touched his life. We find the hard woman of the streets, who had possibly never known anything but simulated love, break down completely before

the One who loved her as a daughter of God.
Even the woman taken in adultery was defended
in her terrible exposure by the Son of God
Himself, and assured that He did not condemn
her.

This method of making people whole by
outflowing love was and is extremely risky, but
it was a risk that Jesus was prepared to take.
And we may infer that God is prepared to take
this the chief risk among all the other risks that
He has taken in giving man free will.

Of course, even the perfect methods of perfect
love did not invariably succeed. But I am draw-
ing attention not to results—much as the modern
world is hypnotised by " results "—but to the
divine method. No doubt, to the early disciples
as they began to realise Who it was that they
were following, the method appeared foolish,
dangerous and even wrong. James and John
were by no means unique in wanting to call
down fire from heaven (St. Luke ix. 54) upon
the village that would not receive incarnate love ;
while, on the other hand, Peter was sharply
rebuked for suggesting that some less dangerous
and less uncompromising way might be found
than the way of vulnerable love in an evil world
(St. Matthew xvi. 23). The single clear purpose

of Christ could never admit that either fire from heaven or the avoiding of suffering could ultimately heal man's evil plight. The methods of Christ, which are the methods of God, are certainly not our normal methods, and if we want to co-operate with His purpose we should do well to study His ways.

(2) The second remarkable fact that emerges from the gospel records is the enmity of the religious. There is a chapter in Professor Jessop's book, *Law and Love*, with the provoking title, " The Badness of Goodness " ; it explains with the utmost clarity the reason why it was not the publicans and sinners, but those whose lifelong purpose was to lead good lives, who, by a strange paradox, became the deadly enemies of God in human form. It is, I think, a mistake to suppose that all the Pharisees, for example, were self-righteous humbugs whose unreality and hypocrisy Jesus mercilessly exposed. It would be truer to say that they were men ruled by principle, often with a great many conspicuous virtues, but they differed from Christ fundamentally in that the mainspring of their lives lay in observing the law and keeping their own souls unspotted from the world, while His lay in loving His Father with the whole of His being, and His fellow men

with the same love that He knew was eternally
at the heart of His Father. Their religion was a
kind of contract, a *quid pro quo* performance,
while His was the spontaneous outliving of
unadulterated love. It must often have looked
to them as though He were ready to drive a
coach and six through the law and the prophets.
But in fact He went far above and beyond any
" righteousness " that the law could produce.
When directly challenged, He declared that the
whole of the prophet's message and the law's
morality depended upon the two most important
commandments, namely, to love God with the
whole of the personality, and to love one's
neighbour as oneself (St. Matthew xxii. 38-40).
St. Paul, seeing the same truth in a slightly
different way—and not, I think, ever quite able,
despite his protestations, to shake himself completely free from the Law in which he was
nurtured—declared, " therefore love is the answer
to the Law's commands " (Romans xiii. 10).

It would be a profound mistake to suppose
that all the Pharisees disappeared soon after the
death of Christ, or that they have no heirs and
successors to-day. Indeed, it is true that there is
much of the Pharisee in each one of us, and by
that I do not mean that we are hypocrites, but

simply that we would rather reduce religion to a code, both inward and outward, than take the tremendous risk of being invaded by and becoming part of vulnerable but relentless love. We do not have to look far to find Christians who have tamed and regulated something that can in fact neither be tamed nor regulated. We do not like risks, we do not like being hurt or disappointed, and there is in us all something of the spirit which would rather label and condemn and bewail than love and suffer and perhaps redeem. We smile as we read of Peter's attempt to regulate the illimitable. He said in effect, " If I have got to forgive, could we not regard seven times as the maximum ? " (St. Matthew xviii. 21). But the same spirit is in us and perhaps we have not yet seen how vast and humble and magnificent and generous is the love of God, nor have we realised that we are to be " perfect, like our Heavenly Father " (St. Matthew v. 48). Yet, until we have some realisation of this illimitable love of God, we shall never understand the conflict between " religion " and the Son of God, observed and recorded for our learning.

(3) The third surprising and rather disquieting side of God's activity while He was on earth

as incarnate love, was His refusal to use supernatural advantages or to interfere with man's
free choice by the use of divine power. We
know for instance that at one period the disciples
confidently expected an earthly kingdom to be
set up, and although their hopes of this became
more and more deferred, yet His death came to
them as a kind of " end-of-the-world " disaster,
so that every loyalty was driven out by their fear
and disappointment. And His appearances after
the Resurrection were to men broken-hearted
and utterly demoralised by the collapse of their
hopes. Despite His constant reminders that His
Kingdom was a spiritual kingdom, it appears
that somehow they expected Him to take the
power and reign. It is true that only one of the
twelve experienced such a bitter reversal of his
hopes that he was prepared to betray the One
he loved for a paltry sum of cash, but of the
others, in their hour of desolation, one denied
him publicly three times, and the others " deserted
him and made their escape " (St. Matthew xxvi.
56 and 70).

I am far from judging the disciples harshly, and
I would be slow to suggest that you and I would
have behaved any differently in the circumstances, but I find the wholesale desertion at the

end of Christ's life an almost certain indication that they could not understand this basic fact about God: that He does not use force to accomplish his purpose. I hope I am not being unduly imaginative when I suggest that it must have crossed their minds many times in those last dark days that it would literally be the easiest thing in the world for God to intervene and prevent the murder of His perfect Son. What a justification of His claims, what a demonstration of the power of light over darkness, what a rousing victory for the God who had visited His people! But no celestial rescue party left the courts of heaven, no angel interfered in the final tragedy. And in the last blackness He cried: " My God, my God, why did You forsake me?" (St. Matthew xxvii. 46).

It is, of course, easy for us to be wise after the event and to know that "all this must take place" (St. Matthew xxvi. 54). But I think it is still true that we are puzzled by the apparent inaction of God. From the crude cry which we heard so often during the war years: "If there is a God, why doesn't He stop Hitler?" to the unspoken questioning in many a Christian heart when a devoted servant of Christ dies from accident or disease at what seems to us a most inopportune moment, there is this universal longing for God to inter-

vene, to show His hand, to vindicate His purpose.
I do not pretend to understand the ways of God
any more than the next man, but it is surely more
fitting as well as more sensible for us to study
what God does do and what He does not do as
He works in and through the complex fabric of
this disintegrated world, than to postulate what
we think God ought to do and then feel demoralised and bitterly disappointed because He fails
to fulfil what we expect of Him. I am certain that
God, who is our Father and understands us perfectly, views, if I may dare to say so, with the
utmost sympathy our desires to see evil dramati-
cally punished, or at least prevented, and good
triumphantly vindicated and conspicuously rewarded. But hard though it is, He has to teach
us that He will no more interfere with other
people's freedom than He does with our own. Yet
I cannot but believe that eventually, most probably in a dimension other than this spatio-
temporal one, we shall understand the final solu-
tion of what are at present incomprehensible
contradictions.

I do not, however, want to leave you with a
picture of a world at the mercy of the evil forces
within it, and into which God never penetrates

because He has promised not to interfere. The true picture is that of a world granted the immense and risky gift of free will, which is at all times surrounded by the love of God. While it is true that God forces His way into no man's personality, yet He is always ready, where the right conditions are fulfilled, to enter and redeem and transform. The chief of the right conditions is what the New Testament calls faith; the willingness to use the faculty which can touch God and which can, as it were, provide an opening through which the ever-present loving purpose can enter and operate. This love may seem to us remote and inactive, but that is because we forget the condition under which it can operate, because we forget its incredible humility, as well as underestimate its true power. Because we all tend to model our ideas of God upon what we see of men, we imagine that He who has the most power will of necessity most obviously demonstrate that power. But if we model our idea of the character of God upon what we see of Jesus Christ, we have a very different picture. We see the astounding humility of God who " stands at the door and knocks " (Revelation iii. 20), and will not enter until he is invited. We see a character not in the least concerned with demonstrations of the kind of power

which impress men superficially, but fully ready to
supply any number of demonstrations of inward
transformation, of arousing love and hope and
enthusiasm, and of providing adequate resources
for carrying through the inward spiritual task.

One further comment: St. John declares that
" every man who truly loves is God's son and
has some knowledge of Him" (1 John iv. 7).
And indeed, a whole sermon could be preached
on that pregnant sentence. But I use it here as
a kind of tailpiece to show that this love of God
of which we have been thinking and of which
so much can be expected, is not so different in
quality that we cannot recognise it as love when
we meet it. It is love, our old familiar friend,
higher and better, more splendid and more
generous, but still love, the most precious thing
that we know, the quality which even in our
duller moments we know can outlast anything.
It is not so much that we do not understand what
love is, but that we are slow to grasp love's
methods of working. We are tempted by love
of power, by the show of results, by the short
cut, by the pleasing exterior; but love is deceived
by none of these things and takes awful patient
ways, of which we know very little. Yet, though
we are blind and ignorant and stupid, it is of

unutterable comfort and gives rise to unspeakable hopes in our hearts to know, not only that
God is wonderful and beautiful and good, but
that He actually is that strange quality which
lives in our inmost heart—love itself.

III

The Work
of Reconciliation

New Testament passages which should be studied in connection with the following chapter are :

2 CORINTHIANS V. VERSES 14 TO THE END

The very spring of our actions is the love of Christ. We look at it like this : if One died for all men then, in a sense, they all died, and His purpose in dying for them is that their lives now should be no longer lived for themselves but for Him Who died and rose again for them. This means that our knowledge of men can no longer be based on their outward lives (indeed, even though we knew Christ as a man we do not know Him like that any longer). For if a man is in Christ he becomes a new person altogether—the past is finished and gone, everything has become fresh and new. All this is God's doing, for He has reconciled us to Himself through Jesus Christ ; and He has made us agents of the reconciliation. God was in Christ personally reconciling the world to Himself—not counting their sins against them—and has commissioned us with the message of reconciliation. We are now Christ's ambassadors, as though God were appealing direct to you through us. As His personal representatives we say, " Make your peace with God." For God caused Christ, Who Himself knew nothing of sin, actually to *be* sin for our sakes, so that in Christ we might be made good with the goodness of God.

2 CORINTHIANS VI.   VERSES I TO 10

As co-operators with God Himself we beg you, then, not to fail to use the grace of God. For God's word is:

> At an acceptable time I hearkened unto thee,
> And in a day of salvation did I succour thee:
> Behold, now is the acceptable time;
> Behold, now is the day of Salvation.

As far as we are concerned we do not wish to stand in anyone's way, nor do we wish to bring discredit on the ministry God has given us. Indeed we want to prove ourselves genuine ministers of God whatever we have to go through—patient endurance of troubles or even disasters, being flogged or imprisoned; being mobbed, having to work like slaves, having to go without food or sleep. All this we want to meet with sincerity, with insight and patience; by sheer kindness and the Holy Spirit; with genuine love, speaking the plain truth, and living by the power of God. Our sole defence, our only weapon, is a life of integrity, whether we meet honour or dishonour, praise or blame. Called "impostors" we must be true, called "nobodies" we must be in the public eye. Never far from death, yet here we are alive, always "going through it" yet never "going under." We know sorrow, yet our joy is inextinguishable. We have "nothing to bless ourselves with," yet we bless many others with true riches. We are penniless, and yet in reality we have everything worth having.

III

THE WORK OF RECONCILIATION

SO FAR we have seen that the love of God, which is " unresting, unhasting, and silent as light " is at all times pressing gently upon the complex and disintegrating scheme of human affairs; that He did, as a matter of sober fact, enter once into the stream of human history as love incarnate in a human being.

He thus began by a kind of personal insertion of Himself a process of integrating men and nations which continues with increasing spiritual momentum to this day. This coming of the light into the darkness was of course no mere " flash in the pan." For wherever men accepted this human figure as the very nature of God expressed in human terms, the same love, the same power of reconciliation and reconstruction became immediately active. Christ Himself said of the man who believes in Him that " he will do even greater things, for I am going away to

the Father " (St. John xiv. 12). There is, I
think, no need to visualise what we call the
Incarnation as a sudden flash of light to be
succeeded thereafter by nothing, but inferior
reflections. It is true that Jesus called Himself
" the Light of the world " (St. John viii. 12),
but using the identical words He also called His
followers " the world's light " (St. Matthew v.
14). And we must not through any false modesty
deny the import of His promise when speaking of His faithful follower—" he will do
the same things that I have done " (St. John
xiv. 12).

Part of the astonishing humility of the love of
God lies, not only in His human level approach
in coming down to where we are, but in His
perfect readiness to use ordinary people like ourselves as channels and instruments in our day
and generation in the vast sweep of His unchanging purpose. We may think it is a proper modesty
on our part to assume that all work done in His
Name must always be inferior in quality and
effect to His own work done upon this earth.
But I believe that by such thinking we are really
belittling His amazing magnanimity and even
cramping the operation of His Spirit, because
we have not properly grasped the generosity of

His purpose. " Here and now," wrote St. John, " we *are* God's children " (1 John iii. 2). This is the kind of truth that we take as being only figuratively true, whereas I am quite certain it is nothing less than an absolute fact, far more true indeed than any " assured result " of scientific investigation. Such a high calling must simultaneously make us swell with pride and fall on our knees in humility.

We must then consider the work of reconciliation which is the initial step towards re-integration, first as begun by the unique work of Christ culminating in the Cross, and then as the work carried through by generation after generation of those who believe in Christ, until we come to our own specific work of reconciliation in our world of to-day.

In speaking of Christ's supreme act of reconciliation, we are, of course, talking of something which can never be repeated, though we know that its never-to-be-forgotten occurrence in time is a visible historical demonstration of the eternal attitude of God. And here, at the risk of appearing to contradict myself, I have to point out that this strange work of Christ is nothing that we ourselves can re-enact. We can and should reproduce the works of Christ since the power and the motive are supplied by His unchanging love, but we are in no position and never could be in a position to build the bridge of reconciliation between the holiness of God and the sinfulness of man. We shall—as we shall see presently—share to some extent in the cost of the working out of reconciliation and redemption, just as St. Paul can say that he is filling up on his part " something of the untold pains which Christ suffers " (Colossians i. 24). But of the strange, awe-full mystery of the Cross, we can bear no part. " God was in Christ personally reconciling the world to himself " (2 Corinthians v. 19). And no one but a fool would think that he could have any part or lot in that infinitely costly work.

Although this is not the occasion to expound theories of the Atonement, it is necessary to stress the *fact* of reconciliation achieved by Christ on the Cross. The theological theories of atonement, held from the days of the early Fathers to the present day, vary enormously, and probably few of us would agree in any exact defining of something which does in fact always elude definition. But we should all agree, and this is of central importance, that at the Cross we are face to face with an action that could only be initiated and carried through by God.

I have already said that Jesus Himself very rarely called men sinners, and He certainly did not attempt deliberately to arouse a sense of guilt. Nevertheless, it is universal for a human being, as he awakens on the God-ward side, to experience a sense of guilt. Almost every religion bears testimony to this world-wide sense of human failure, and there are many pathetic and desperate attempts to close the gap that man's sin has made between himself and God. In a so-called civilised country, the primitive sense of guilt and the need for reconciliation is often over-laid or even deeply buried. But those of us who deal with the problems of human souls know that sooner or later this basic need is sure to show itself. And millions have found, as they accept the supreme sacrifice of the Cross, that the haunting sense that " something ought to be done about it " is by this act miraculously set at rest. What we feel ought to be done, but what we know we could never do, we find *has been done* through this mysterious sacrifice. At the most the human soul can only construct a desperate bridgehead towards God, but the gulf remains unspanned. Yet in Christ we sense intuitively, even perhaps super-rationally, that the bridge has been well and truly built and that through Him we have access to the Father (Romans v. 2, and Ephesians ii. 18, and iii. 12). Moreover, the act takes on a personal significance as the soul awakens to God. " The Son of God, who loved me and sacrificed Himself for me " (Galatians ii. 20), wrote St. Paul, though he would have been the first to declare that the act of reconciliation was designed to reconcile all men to God.

When we think of Christ's positive approach, does it not seem that some Christians go about their work of reconciliation with the wrong emphasis ? They are convinced—and of course they are perfectly right—that the Cross of Christ is God's answer to the sin of man. They do all they can to arouse and foster a sense of sin. Consciously or unconsciously, they try to make people feel guilty, and then they consider it is not very difficult to point them to the demonstration and means of forgiveness. I am not at all sure that this is sound psychology or sound evangelism.

It is evident from the Gospels that the appeal of Jesus Christ was an appeal to the real man who lives in each personality, covered and defended as that real self may be by pretences and disguises, to follow Him. It is a positive and not a negative appeal, and though common sense alone tells us that He realised far more deeply than we ever could how effective a barrier was man's sin between himself and God, yet He does not seek deliberately to arouse the sense of sin. Of course, men felt it ; of course their unreality was challenged and exposed by His reality ; of course their self-love and their disguise gradually or suddenly became apparent in the light of the simplicity of His self-giving love. But His work of reconciliation began and ended in positive and active love. He knew very well that He alone could make the reconciliation between man and God, because He alone was both perfect man and perfect God. He was prepared to allow the forces of evil to close in upon Him and kill Him ; He was prepared to " taste death for every man " (Hebrews ii. 9). He who knew no sin was prepared " actually to *be* sin for our sakes " (2 Corinthians v. 21)—an experience which wrung from Him that bitter cry from the Cross : " My God, my God, why did You forsake me ? " (St. Matthew xxvii. 46).

Yet how little did Christ advertise or even mention, even to His closest disciples, the

appalling depth to which He must plunge to win
men to God. It is as though love was more
important than the action of love, however fear-
ful and far-reaching in consequence the ultimate
sacrifice might be. If I may use a human illustration to reflect most imperfectly my feeling on
this matter : a man who has rescued his friend
from death at great personal risk, does not need,
nor does he feel inclined, to bring up the matter
every time they meet! Or to take a further human
illustration : you and I are living to-day in
freedom because during the late war other men
gave their lives, their health, their sight, even
their sanity for our liberty. Now whether we like
it or not, whether we believe it or not, or even
whether we know it or not, we are free because
of them. To an infinitely greater and more permanent degree the unique sacrifice of Christ has
changed the relationship between man and God.
Whether a man knows it and feels it or not, the
first stupendous step has been irreversibly taken
and the world can never be the same again since
God was in Christ reconciling the world unto
Himself. Men may be slow and blind, or obstinate
and rebellious, but the reconciliation is potentially
true already. And because of this, Jesus Christ
had no need to underline man's sin, but rather

to declare to them and to live out the selfless love of God.

The Cross of Christ is indeed the focal point, patent as historical fact, of the vast sweep of God's work of reconciliation, for in this central act the man with eyes to see can observe the devastating humility of God. Not only did God in the person of Christ make what C. S. Lewis calls " that tremendous dive " and become one of ourselves, but He accepted the unspeakable disgrace, the horror and the darkness, that lie behind the Cross of Calvary. Yet I must repeat that the reconciliation of the Cross is but the outcrop in human history of a vast, invisible, unforgettable purpose—the love of God—" personally reconciling the world unto Himself—not counting their sins against them " (2 Corinthians v. 19). Backwards in time from this unforgettable act, as well as forwards, the steady pressure of reconciliation is for ever at work. And we who are lovers and followers of Christ are commissioned with the " message of reconciliation " (2 Corinthians v. 19). Amazing as it seems, and amazing as indeed it is, we who are reconciled to God through Christ are now the living agents, the local representatives, of the celestial task of

making men both reconciled and whole. " Just
as the Father sent me," said Jesus to His early
followers, " so I am now going to send you "
(St. John xx. 21). He makes no distinction. The
reconciling, whole-making energy and purpose
of love which was in Him is to be in us as
well, for " We realise that our life in this
world is actually His life lived in us " (1 John
iv. 17).

It is both sensible and salutary to reflect on
this high calling. So often we are bogged down
by consideration of our own soul's welfare, or
bedevilled by the thought of our own unworthi-
ness, that we fail to see the greatness of our
calling as sons of God and ministers of reconciliation. Fortunately for us we learn by doing,
even by failing, so that we have not to wait until
we have reached some fantastic height of spiritual
fitness before God can use us. Provided that we
have accepted His act of reconciliation, and have
dropped our attempts to justify ourselves we
are embarked, however imperfectly, upon the
ministry of reconciliation, upon the task of
making men whole. We can truthfully say, with
bated breath if you like, that we are " co-
operators with God Himself " (2 Corinthians
vi. 1).

It would, of course, be the height of impertinence for any man to suggest that he could bear the smallest part in " Christ's strange work " of reconciliation. That work was unique in that it could only be accomplished by God-become-Man. Yet it is true that in carrying out the work of Christ there is an inescapable cost and pain to be borne, which is in a rather different sense the price of redemption. To follow Christ does indeed mean for every man taking up " his cross every day " (St. Luke ix. 23); and the carrying of that cross as a symbol, not merely of the denial of the selfish way of living, but of a certain humble sharing of the price that must be paid in bringing truth face to face with falsehood, healing into contact with disease, wholeness to a world rebellious and awry. We are, as God's " ambassadors," not merely commissioned to proclaim the divine appeal, " make your peace with God " (2 Corinthians v. 20), but cheerfully and constantly to bear our share of the cost of that work of reconciliation. In all humility we can say that, at any rate in a limited sense, God is in every true Christian " personally reconciling the world to Himself."

We follow different vocations and the particular pain and cost of our part in the work of making men whole will naturally be different too. The teacher, especially the teacher abroad, has to cope with ignorance and possibly with the darkness and dull apathy which are the fruit of centuries. There is no need for me to point out to teachers that the cost of all true teaching is a high demand upon the personality of the teacher. But the very demands that good teaching makes are the measure of its value in the purpose of God, who in this particular operation of His Spirit is bringing light into darkness and order into muddle and indiscipline.

Again, the doctor and the nurse need no underlining from me of the cost of their profession. They are always in the front line of a particular battle, and since the psychological aspect of healing is coming to be recognised more and more, so it becomes less and less possible to draw a hard and fast line between the healing of the body and the healing of the whole man. Although I believe, arguing from the innumerable works of healing of our Lord Himself, that sickness and disease are never in themselves the will of God, yet their incidence is often a sharp and salutary reminder of our mortal frailty and of our complete dependence upon the laws of the Creator. It would be an unwarrantable exaggeration to claim that the sickness of the body invariably provides a spiritual opportunity ; but it is true to say that in the healing and care of the sick and diseased there is an opportunity of mediating the wholeness of Christ in a way which is peculiarly intimate and memorable.

The work of the pastor of human souls is a vocation about which I naturally know rather more. And here, if we are as Christ was, " gentle and humble in heart " (St. Matthew xi. 29) the cost is often high. To listen patiently, to use skilfully imaginative sympathy, to advise wisely —these things all carry something of the price of redemption. Those of us who try not only to sort out human muddles but to strip away misconceptions and prejudices which prevent the soul from seeing its God, know that we have a work with its own peculiar tears and toil and sweat. The preacher and the writer may seem to have an apparently easy task. At first sight it may seem that they have only to proclaim and declare, but in fact, if their words are to enter men's hearts and bear fruit, they must be the right words shaped cunningly to pass men's defences and explode silently and effectually within their minds. This means in practice turning a face of flint towards the easy cliché,

the well-worn religious cant and phraseology,
dear no doubt to the faithful but utterly meaning-
less to those outside the fold. It means learning
how people are thinking and how they are
feeling ; it means learning with patience, imagination and ingenuity the way to pierce apathy or
blank lack of understanding. I sometimes
wonder what hours of prayer and thought lie
behind the apparently simple and spontaneous
parables of the Gospels. It is not enough for us
who are preachers or writers to give an adequate
performance before the eyes and ears of our
fellow writers and preachers ; instead we have
the formidable task of reconciling the Word of
truth with the thought-forms of a people
estranged from God ; interpreting without
changing or diluting the essential Word.

These are but a few examples from our many
callings, each with its particular cost. " Men
have different gifts, but it is the same Spirit Who
gives them " (1 Corinthians xii. 4) ; the measure-
less varieties of God's wisdom are at work in
them all. Doubtless there are times when we all
bewail the particular pains and distresses of our
calling, and even think enviously of someone
else's vocation, but the plain fact is that if we
are called of God to bear a part in His purpose,

there can be no evasion of its cost. I do not suppose a little good-tempered " moaning " is particularly offensive to God. Indeed, Christ Himself once sighed wearily : " Oh, what a faithless people you are ! How long must I be with you before you will believe ; how long must I bear your lack of faith ? " (St. Mark ix. 19). But it is of great importance, indeed it is essential to our life as Christians, that we should recognise cheerfully and realistically that no worthwhile work is accomplished without patience and sacrifice ; and, more important still, that we should realise with a sudden quickening of the pulses that the cost we bear is, not a kind of occupational nuisance, but the honour of sharing God's cost in bringing men to Himself and changing them from wayward human beings into sons of Himself.

Let us then be clear what is involved in making our vocation serve God's purpose of reconciliation. Christianity is full of joy, but it is not a joy-ride. Christ was, I believe, full of humour, but He was inescapably " a man of sorrows " (Isaiah liii. 3). It is as if we were called to be, as Sir Winston Churchill said in one of the darkest hours of the late world war, both grim and gay. The grimness comes from our knowledge of the

strength of the forces arrayed against us : the
stubbornness of human self-will, the sheer dead
weight of apathy which above all else would
quench the fires of our spirit. But gay we must
be too, because day by day we have the deepest
satisfaction this world can afford, of knowing
that we are co-operating with—and even being
allowed to share the cost of—the purpose of
God Himself.

Of course we often feel discouraged. We think
of our high calling and are dismayed at the
meagre response to our labour. We see, in a
kind of indelible vision, the unfailing, reconciling
purpose of God, and we are surrounded by
thousands who see no such thing. For all our
labours, for all our heartbreak and our pain, we
have so little to show. The remedy is to " think
constantly of Him " (Hebrews xii. 3), and not to
lash ourselves with useless feelings of guilt,
failure and frustration. Consider Him. Was He,
incarnate love in person, a success ? Should we,
if we did not know the answer already, consider
His mission successful, when at the time of crisis
" all the disciples deserted him, and made their
escape " ? (St. Matthew xxvi. 56).   Are we
expecting more favourable results than He
achieved ? Or are we prepared, as He was, to

" dare to take the awful patient ways of God " and be content to do the Father's will?

We must not be infected by the world's valuations of either speed or success. The responsibilities which faced Christ as a human being would be, if we stop to think, enough to drive the most balanced man out of his mind. But He maintained His poise, His joy and His peace. He did the Father's will; and that is both the most and the highest that we can do.

IV

Inner Resources for the Task

New Testament passages which should be studied in connection with the following chapter are :

I JOHN III.   VERSES 1 TO 10

Consider the incredible love that the Father has shown us in allowing us to be called " children of God "—and that is not just what we are called, but what we *are*. Our heredity on the God-ward side is no mere figure of speech —which explains why the world will no more recognise us than it recognised Christ.

Oh, dear children of mine (forgive the affection of an old man !), have you realised it ? Here and now we *are* God's children. We don't know what we shall become in the future. We only know that, if reality were to break through we should reflect His likeness, for we should see Him as He really is.

Everyone who has at heart a hope like that keeps himself pure, for he knows how pure Christ is.

Everyone who commits sin breaks God's law, for that is what sin is, by definition—a breaking of God's law. You know, moreover, that Christ became Man for the purpose of removing sin, and that He Himself was quite free from sin. The man who lives " in Christ " does not habitually sin. The regular sinner has never seen or known Him. You, my children, are younger than I am, and I don't want you to be taken in by any clever talk just here. The man who lives a consistently good life is a good man, as surely as God is good. But the man whose life is habitually sinful is spiritually a son of the devil, for

the devil is behind all sin, as he always has been. Now
the Son of God came to earth with the express purpose of
liquidating the devil's activities. The man who is really
God's son does not practise sin, for God's nature is
in him, for good, and such a heredity is incapable of
sin.

Here we have a clear indication as to who are the
children of God and who are the children of the devil.
The man who does not lead a good life is no son
of God, and neither is the man who fails to love his
brother.

GALATIONS III.   VERSES 26 TO THE END

For now that you have faith in Christ you are all sons of
God. All of you who were baptised " into " Christ have
put on the family likeness of Christ. Gone is the distinction between Jew and Greek, slave and free man, male
and female—you are all one in Christ Jesus ! And if you
belong to Christ, you are true descendants of Abraham,
you are true heirs of his Promise.

GALATIANS IV.   VERSES 1 TO 7

But you must realise that so long as an heir is a child,
though he is destined to be master of everything, he is, in
practice, no different from a servant. He has to obey a
guardian or trustee until the time which his father has
chosen for him to receive his inheritance. So is it with
us : while we were " children " we lived under the
authority of basic moral principles. But when the proper
time came God sent His Son, born of a human mother
and born under the jurisdiction of the Law, that He might
redeem those who were under the authority of the Law

and lead us into becoming, by adoption, true sons of God. It is because you really are His sons that God has sent the Spirit of His Son into your hearts to cry "Father, dear Father." You my brother, are not a servant any longer; you are a *son*. And if you are a son, then you are certainly an heir of God through Christ.

IV

INNER RESOURCES FOR THE TASK

As WE grow up, our minds develop in a score of different ways. Our experience and our insight into people, ideas, and problems grow deeper. At the same time, unless we have allowed ourselves to become bogged down by some rigidity in our religious thinking, our ideas of God expand greatly, and there come times when we realise with an awe-struck humility that what we once worshipped as God was only, so to speak, the shimmering hem of His garment. If we are foolish we cling with desperate loyalty to the limited conception of God that we have at present, but if we are wise, we " launch out into the deep " (St. Luke v. 4, *A.V.*), and allow every true experience of life, every touch or sight of goodness, truth and beauty, to open fresh windows upon the illimitable magnificence of God. We cannot hold too big a conception of God, but the more our hearts and minds and imaginations are used, the more astounding becomes the central fact of our faith—that so infinite a God allowed Himself to be, so to speak, scaled down to fit the narrow limits of humanity. For all His vastness and mystery, He has made Himself known in an unforgettable character by which all men can see what sort of a Person it is " with Whom we have to do " (Hebrews iv. 13). It is as though, having once accepted this tremendous fact, we view all that we can see or discover of the complex wisdom of God through a Christ-shaped aperture.

This much we see as our experience unfolds, and there also expands before our minds the " one increasing purpose." What may well have come to each one of us personally as an experience of Christ is seen to be a tiny part of a vast pattern and plan of redemption embracing men of every race and colour, requiring centuries for its operation in time, and having always as its source and background the timeless life of eternity.

Beneath the vast sweep of the divine plan, we who are followers of Christ Jesus see ourselves as both humble and uplifted. We are humbled because at the very most we can only play a tiny part in the great scheme of salvation, and, as our

Lord once pointed out (with a smile, I imagine), when we have done all we can still only reflect that " we are not much good as servants " (St. Luke xvii. 10). At the same time we are uplifted because through the incredible generosity of God, we are called in our day and generation to take part in this tremendous purpose ; and, more than that, made His sons, not figuratively but actually sons of God, who " share His treasures " (Romans viii. 17).

As we look at the world with adult eyes, by far the most important thing in life plainly becomes this grand scheme of reconciliation and redemption. And for ourselves the most important thing is to be sure that we are taking our full part—whatever the vocation to which we are called—in working together with God.

Such a high and tremendous task could easily fill us with despair if it were not for the fact that it is God Himself " Who is at work within you, giving you the will and the power to achieve His purpose " (Philippians ii. 13). We have thought already of the immensity of God outside us, what is known technically as the transcendence of God ; but what is so often lacking in present-day Christians is an adequate sense of God within us, that is, what is known technically as the immanence of God. Unhappily in our day the Christian religion is all too often reduced to a performance to please an external God, while to the early Christians it was plainly the invasion of their lives by a new quality of life—nothing less than the life of God Himself. I believe this lack of faith in God-within-us is largely unconscious, for while we should be the first to recognise that lack of faith on man's part inhibited even the powers of Christ Himself, yet I do not think we realise that this same lack of faith in Christ-within-us prevents the operation of His power, and our proper development as sons of God. There is far too much strenuous, even hysterical, effort, and far too little quiet confidence in the Christ within us. Certainly Christians admit that they need the help of God in the tasks to which they are called, and certainly they seek it. But I have an uneasy feeling that many do not really believe that God Himself actually operates within their personalities. It is almost as though they visualise themselves like Christians in *Pilgrim's Progress*, as treading a dangerous and narrow path and winning the Celestial City only by the skin of their teeth. I doubt very much whether they see themselves as sons and daughters of the Most High, not merely receiving occasional help from God, but continually and without intermission indwelt by the living Spirit of God.

In the experience of St. Paul and his followers, the revolutionary thought—" that sacred mystery which up till now has been hidden in every age and every generation " (Colossians i. 26)—is that God is no longer the external power and authority, but One who lives *in* them, transforming their thinking and feeling, renewing their minds, inspiring their hearts, and effectually preventing them from being conformed to this fleeting world.   Such a conviction is indeed revolutionary, and we may well ask ourselves whether this revolution in thought has taken place effectually within each one of us ; for so long as we do not really believe this truth in our heart of hearts, it remains a theological idea or a beautiful thought and has no noticeable effect upon our lives.

Startling results are bound to follow in human life once the truth is accepted that God actually lives in and operates through personality.   In considering some of them I am not going to be unduly bothered by theological accuracy, any more than it seems to me St. Paul was concerned with Trinitarian exactitude !   He talks freely of

God being in people, of Christ being in people, and of the Spirit being in people, and I think it would be most unfair to his spontaneous writings to try to read back into them any theological implications in his varied usage. God is one God, and although we have evolved the doctrine of the Blessed Trinity in order to safeguard the truths that we know about God against inadequate and false conceptions, yet I am sure that when we are considering the actual fact of God living in us, to be theologically scrupulous is beside the point. We could, after all, be quite meticulous in theological expression and yet never really accept the fact that the infinite God is alive and powerful within every Christian.

I begin then by mentioning a startling sentence from St. John's first Epistle. It reads like this in the Authorised Version : " Whosoever is begotten of God doeth no sin because his seed abideth in him ; and he cannot sin because he is begotten of God " (1 John iii. 9). As we think into it we shall find that this is an altogether staggering sentence, meaning, I am sure, that the Christian is able not to sin because " God's seed remaineth in him " ; or, if we change it into modern idiom, *because God's heredity is in him for good*. This is one of the revealed truths of God

which many Christians are inclined to take with
a grain of salt, thereby robbing it of any real
effectiveness. I believe it to be not only true but
perfectly reasonable and logical. For if we are,
through Christ, sons of God, that is to say, not
sons of God by courtesy title but really sons of
God, there must be in us something of the
heredity of God. Plainly this heredity we derive
from Him is both incapable of sin and able not
to sin. And it is a factor upon which we can
reckon with every confidence. It is, of course,
true that there are other factors within us, of
which we are only too well aware and which to
my mind are often unduly stressed. Indeed I
think we do ourselves and God a disservice by
continually harping upon our own sinfulness.
We do very much more good if we honestly
believe and reckon upon our capacity, through
Christ, of sinlessness. So often one has heard
Christians taking an almost morbid delight in
their discoveries of their own sinfulness, yet how
rarely has one heard of Christians delighting in
their own God-given capacity not to sin. God's
heredity is in you and me, a potent and in the
last resort undefeatable factor in our personalities.
Just as surely as human traits of character will
" come out " in our children, so surely will the

likeness of Christ be exhibited in those who are
God's sons through Him.

We are slow to believe this, and we tend to
play it down as though it were somehow presumptuous on our part to believe that the very
nature of God is in us. We may, and we should,
feel unworthy of such high honour, but the
whole glory and beauty of the Gospel is that it
is God's free gift. There is no question here of
deserving—nobody deserves this gift of God.
There is no question of being worthy, for no one
is worthy of such an honour. It is all part of
God's amazing generosity that in order to make
His vast plan of reconciliation practicable through
frail and often unreliable human agents, He not
only calls them sons of God, but makes them
sons of God. He does not give them a mere
tantalising title; He implants a dependable
heredity within them.

The continual unremitting work of the Spirit
within us—if we give Him the right conditions
in which to work—is to change us into becoming
quite naturally, and as a matter of course, sons
of God. The attractive fruits of the Spirit which
St. Paul lists in Galatians v. 22-23 are real fruits.
They are indeed supernaturally produced, but
they are not supernatural qualities. The love,

joy, peace, which St. Paul had observed in the
lives of those who were open on the God-ward
side are easily recognisable as human qualities,
*and yet they are the very qualities of which human
nature without Christ so quickly runs short.* We
almost automatically assume that these are not
fruits at all but accomplishments produced by
strenuous labour and stern self-denial. But in
fact I am convinced that they are the outward
and visible signs of the indwelling of human
personalities by the living Spirit of God. I have
already spoken of that horrid thing, love in
inverted commas, but so long as we regard the
Christian religion as a performance instead of an
experience, we shall tend to produce, not only
love, but joy, peace, long-suffering and all the
rest as artificial attitudes, or at the most hot-
house fruit. This again is because we impose
upon ourselves standards and restrictions instead
of being inwardly free and relaxed in the liberty
of the Spirit. " Consider how the wild flowers
grow. They neither work nor weave, but I tell
you that even Solomon in all his glory was not
arrayed like one of these! " (St. Matthew vi.
28-29). The spontaneous natural flower and
fruit of a life open to the Spirit of God is as
much to be preferred to the tense, over-anxious

performance of Christian values, as the beauty of the wild flower is superior to Solomon's imposing magnificence.

All this may seem strange and even a little fantastic to us to-day, because we are infected far more than we know by the closed-system mode of thought by which we are surrounded. The world in its wisdom has learned many things through the centuries, but particularly through the last fifty years man has come to regard all the complexity of this life as a self-contained system in which " cause and effect " can be shown to be responsible for all phenomena. We know more and more of the laws which govern the cause and effect, but less and less are we inclined to believe that there can be any penetration of this closed world by anybody or anything from outside. This way of thinking has affected us far more than we realise, and consequently we are not only much slower to believe in the power of God and in these breath-taking promises and gifts in which the New Testament specialises, but our whole personalities have grown closed and insensitive on the God-ward side.

The unpleasant price we pay for this know-all attitude is, of course, for the ordinary man of the world the blankest materialism, while for the Christian, as we have seen already, it reduces a dynamic living faith to a rather wearisome performance. We need to make a really determined effort of faith to break through this crust of modern unbelief, and to recapture that New Testament attitude of mind by which God is confidently reckoned upon to provide the necessities for the new life. We can, alas, so easily reflect wistfully that " times were different then," and thus excuse ourselves from the consequence of believing in a God alive and active to-day. It is true that times were different then, but I think we can be quite certain that, although the enemies and hindrances of the early Church were different from ours, they were certainly not less. The Christian faith took root and flourished in an atmosphere almost entirely pagan where cruelty and sexual immorality were taken for granted, where slavery and the inferiority of women were universally accepted, while superstitions, cults and contending religions, with all kinds of bogus claims, existed on every hand.

Within this pagan mess the early Christians, by the power of God within them, lived their lives as His sons. They were pioneers of the new humanity, they showed for all the world to see the fruits of the Spirit in human life. At times the opposition was almost overwhelming, as we can glimpse from St. Paul's second letter to the Corinthians, chapter iv. verses 5 to 10:

For it is Christ Jesus the Lord Whom we preach, not ourselves; we are your servants for His sake. God, Who first ordered Light to shine in darkness has flooded our hearts with His Light. We now can enlighten men only because we can give them knowledge of the glory of God, as we see it in the face of Jesus Christ.

This priceless treasure we hold, so to speak, in a common earthenware jar—to show that the splendid power of it belongs to God and not to us. We are handicapped on all sides, but we are never frustrated; we are puzzled, but never in despair. We are persecuted, but we never have to stand it alone; we may be knocked down but we are never knocked out! Every day we experience something of the death of the Lord Jesus, so that we may also know the power of the life of Jesus in these bodies of ours.

M.W.   D

Now the reason for the significant "buts" in that passage is not the personal courage of St. Paul, as he would have been the first to point out, but the Christ who lived in him, as He does in all true Christians.

To-day we face a very different world, though to analyse even briefly the particular anti-Christian elements of our surroundings is not my purpose here. But the moment that we accept seriously, and by that I do not mean solemnly, Jesus Christ as Lord, we find both within us and without us a dead and depressing weight of opposition. It is depressing because it is not as a rule violent hostility, but a soul-destroying apathy, aptly epitomised by that truly horrifying expression "I couldn't care less." And it is within us as well, because the fog of prevailing unbelief has seeped into many Christian lives and choked their joy and confidence.

Now this is where I believe we have got to do battle, and to battle first with that refusal to believe which has resulted in the atrophy of the faith-faculty, and which has become so habitual as to be part and parcel of our lives. Looking aside for a moment from the revealed Word of God, can we not see the utter absurdity of God's expecting us little impotent human beings to

live as His sons, His representatives, His ambassadors, unless He guarantees and provides
constantly the power so to believe and so to
behave. If Christian living is to be the instrument
of God's purpose of making men whole, it must
provide a supernatural quality of life; there
must be an invasion of ordinary human life by
God Himself. If God's plan is to have the
remotest chance of success, then He must provide
supernaturally joy and peace and love and
courage and patience, and all the other virtues
which we so deeply need. I say, " He *must*,"
for that seems to me to be merely logical and
sensible. And if we turn to the Epistles of the
New Testament, which are for the most part
our earliest Christian documents, we find plenty
of evidence of this very thing—God pouring
into ordinary lives those extra qualities which
the sons of God need for their living. Some
phrases leap at once to the mind :

Strengthened from God's bound-
    less resources ..   ..   ..   (Colossians i. 11)
Filled through all your being
    with God Himself ..   ..   (Ephesians iii. 19)
May the God of hope fill you
    with joy and peace in your
    faith, that by the power of the
    Holy Spirit, your whole life

and outlook may be radiant
with hope   ..   ..   ..   (Romans xv. 13)
Able to resist evil in its day of
power ..   ..   (Ephesians vi. 13)
Blameless, sincere and whole-
some, living in a warped and
diseased world   (Philippians ii. 15)

There are, of course, many more. But can we in all honesty say that such expressions accurately describe our own experience of the power of God within us? Of course we know something of these qualities, and possibly we dream a little wistfully of how one day perhaps they might be true of us. I am quite convinced that they are meant to be true here and now for all those who in heart and mind are allied to the eternal purpose. It is laughable even to suggest that God has changed with the passing centuries or that His resources of spiritual power have somehow petered out, and yet *that is often exactly what our lives imply.*

Now when we begin to recover our faith in God alive within us, we cannot help being conscious of His purpose both within us and through us. The working out of that purpose is vast and varied, and besides the equipment already mentioned—adequate power for the job in hand to live as sons of God despite the outward circumstances, and spontaneously to produce those overflowing virtues which we call the fruits of the Spirit—we will consider two particular activities of God within us which are of very great importance.

The first is the ability to think and feel according to the mind of Christ, and to remain unaffected by the prevailing climate of opinion. In writing to the Romans, St. Paul once said : " Be not conformed to this world : but be ye transformed by the renewing of your mind " (Romans xii. 2, A.V.). Notice that he does not say, " transform yourselves," but allow yourselves to be transformed. The world inevitably tends to make people conform in their thinking and feeling to its habit and outlook, to its own pattern. The man who lacks inner resources and a vision of God will inevitably, sooner or later, conform to the contemporary pressures. We see it happening before our eyes. Modern materialism has already produced the mass-mind.

But to St. Paul at least there is an immensely potent factor working in the opposite direction, the moulding of man's character and outlook from within. This to him was nothing less than

the ever present, ever fresh, ever new, Spirit of
God Himself, well able not merely to counteract
the pressures of the surrounding world, but to
renew and rearm in spite of it. Nor does St.
Paul regard this inward power as a mere balancing
force which enables a man to retain his spiritual
balance and nothing more. " No, we win an
overwhelming victory through Him Who has
proved His love for us " (Romans viii. 37). The
power is far more than enough to keep a man
in spiritual health; it spills over; it is the
Spirit of love and power as well as of a sound
mind (2 Timothy i. 7). We can be confident that
St. Paul whose experience of life was both deep
and varied, knew what he was talking about here,
and we can rely on his evidence of observed
spiritual power in human life. Pressed as we are
by an unbelieving and often apathetic world, we
all need to see ourselves transformed by the
renewing of our minds by the same Spirit. Do
we believe that to be possible in this year of
grace ?

The second activity of the Spirit which seems
to me to be pressing more and more upon the
consciousness of Christians is His unifying purpose. To quote St. Paul again : " Gone is the
distinction between Jew and Greek, slave and

free man, male and female—you are all one in
Christ Jesus " (Galatians iii. 28).   It is not
within my special province to speak of the
heightening of racial tensions on the one hand,
or the breaking down of prejudices on the other.
Such a subject needs expert treatment.   Nor am
I qualified to speak except as an ordinary parish
priest of the deep and growing desire for unity
in Christ which is expressing itself on all hands,
while at the same time die-hards of various parties
are putting up what we may hope are their last
defences.   But anyone with half an eye can see
that there is beginning to emerge a new sense
of common humanity on the one hand, and at
the same time a steadily increasing pressure
towards unity within the Church itself.

It would be fascinating to explore the possible
inter-relation of these two phenomena of our
day.   While I have neither the knowledge nor
the experience to do that, it is at least possible
to surmise that both these movements are taking
place under the gentle but insistent pressure of
the same Spirit.   I am a firm believer in what I
may perhaps call the extra-mural work of God's
Spirit, and it would not surprise me to find that
in His passion for the wholeness of all His
creatures, God is bringing about, by any and

every means that He may use under the limits
that He has set Himself, the unity of mankind.
There is a school of psychology which advances
the attractive hypothesis that all men share a
common unconscious mind, and that they are
therefore linked in one beneath the level of what
we call personality. This may or may not be
true. But it is most certainly true of those who
through Christ are the sons of God. At all times
they are brothers; at all times they share the
family likeness, and together they comprise the
" one new man " which St. Paul had seen as it
were in embryo. It is said to be a mark of
maturity to recognise ever more fully our
common humanity with our fellows, and that, I
think, is true. Surely the Christian, the son of
God, indwelt by God, transformed in heart and
mind by the God who lives within Him, the
pioneer of the new humanity, should be the first
to realise what the Spirit is driving at—the
making whole of all men in Christ.

V

Completeness in Christ :
In Time and in Eternity

New Testament passages which should be studied in connection with the following chapter are :

I CORINTHIANS XII.   VERSES 4 TO 27

Men have different gifts, but it is the same Spirit Who gives them. There are different ways of serving God, but it is the same Lord Who is served. God works through different men in different ways, but it is the same God Who achieves His purposes through them all. Each man is given his gift by the Spirit that he may make the most of it.

One man's gift by the Spirit is to speak with wisdom, another's to speak with knowledge. The same Spirit gives to another man faith, to another the ability to heal, to another the power to do great deeds. The same Spirit gives to another man the gift of preaching the word of God, to another the ability to discriminate in spiritual matters, to another speech in different tongues and to yet another the power to interpret the tongues. Behind all these gifts is the operation of the same Spirit, Who distributes to each individual man, as He wills.

As the human body, which has many parts, is a unity, and those parts despite their multiplicity, comprise together one single body, so it is with the Body of Christ. For we were all baptised by the Spirit into one Body, whether we were Jews, Gentiles, slaves or free men, and we have all had experience of the same spirit.

Now the body is not one member but many. If the foot should say, " Because I am not a hand I don't belong to the body," does that alter the fact that the foot *is* a part

of the body? Or if the ear should say, "Because I am
not an eye I don't belong to the body," does that mean
that the ear really is no part of the body? After all, if
the body were all one Eye, for example, where would be
the sense of hearing? Or if it were all one Ear, where
would be the sense of smell? But God has arranged all
the parts in the one body, according to His design. So
that the eye cannot say to the hand, "I don't need you!"
nor, again, can the head say to the feet, "I don't need
you!" On the contrary, those parts of the body which
have no obvious function are the more essential to health;
and to those parts of the body which seem to us to be
less deserving of notice we have to allow the highest
honour of function. The parts which do not look beautiful
have a deeper beauty in the work they do, while the parts
that look beautiful may not be at all essential to life! But
God has harmonised the whole body by giving importance
of function to the parts which lack apparent importance,
that the body should work together as a whole with all
the members in sympathetic relationship with one another.
So it happens that if one member suffers all the other
members suffer with it, and if one member is honoured
all the members share a common joy.

Now you are together the Body of Christ, and indi-
vidually you are members of Him.

2 CORINTHIANS IV. VERSES 16 TO THE END

This is the reason why we never collapse. The outward
man does indeed suffer wear and tear, but every day the
inward man receives fresh strength. These little troubles
(which are really so transitory) are winning for us a permanent and glorious reward out of all proportion to our
pain. For we are looking all the time not at the visible

things but at the invisible. The visible things are transitory: it is the invisible things that are really permanent.

2 CORINTHIANS V. VERSES 1 TO 10

We know, for instance, that if our earthly dwelling were taken down, like a tent, we have a permanent house in Heaven, made, not by man, but by God. In this present frame we sigh with deep longing for the heavenly house, for we do not want to face utter nakedness when death destroys our present dwelling—these bodies of ours. So long as we are clothed in this temporary dwelling we have a painful longing, not because we want just to get rid of these " clothes " but because we want to know the full cover of the permanent house that will be ours. We want our transitory life to be absorbed into the Life that is eternal.

Now the power that has planned this experience for us is God, and He has given us His Spirit as a guarantee of its truth. This makes us confident, whatever happens. We realise that being " at home " in the body means that to some extent we are " away " from the Lord, for we have to live by trusting Him without seeing Him. We are so sure of this that we would really rather be " away " from the body and be " at home " with the Lord.

It is our aim, therefore, to please Him, whether we are " at home " or " away." For every one of us will have to stand without pretence before Christ our Judge, and we shall be rewarded for what we did when we lived in our bodies, whether it was good or bad.

V

COMPLETENESS IN CHRIST:
IN TIME AND IN ETERNITY

IN VARYING degree we achieve a mental and
spiritual vision of the vast scale of the operation
by which God intends to establish His purpose
of wholeness in this disintegrated and disrupted
world. From our present limited point of view
this will always seem not only a slow but even
an inefficient process. Once we have accepted
what we believe to be factually true, and have
grasped the purpose behind the Spirit's constant
movement, we are tortured, or at least continually irritated, by the contrast between what
we observe happening in the world, and what
we believe, and indeed can see in imagination,
could and should happen if the rule of Christ
were accepted. If we are enthusiastic, we are
continually tempted to force the pace, and it is
perhaps salutary to remind ourselves that although
we understand to some extent the great increasing
purpose, yet it will always remain somewhat

mysterious, inexplicable and indeed unsatis-
factory to our natural minds. This is particularly
true in an age such as ours which is hag-ridden
by regulations, forms, numbers, Gallup-polls,
statistics and every other modern device which
tries to rationalise and regularise the complex
factors of human life.

There is an apparent capriciousness and arbitrariness about the working of the Spirit of God
which laughs at our modern docketing. The
Spirit, like the wind, said Jesus, " blows where
it likes " (St. John iii. 8), and though we can
fulfil conditions and, so to speak, set our sails
to meet the wind of the Spirit, yet (to change
the metaphor) we can never harness or organise
the living Spirit of God. We are indeed sure
of His gentle purpose, but the details of His
plan lie beyond our understanding and it is
at once more sensible and more fitting for us
to cultivate a sensitivity to the leading of the
Spirit, rather than to arrange His work for
Him !

This unpredictable and supra-rational movement of the Spirit is an element in God's working
which makes the whole Christian enterprise on
which we are engaged at once more exciting and

more difficult. " In Elijah's time . . . there were
plenty of widows in Israel, but Elijah was not
sent to any of them. But he *was* sent to Sarepta,
to a widow in the country of Sidon," said Jesus
(St. Luke iv. 25-26), and He offered no comment
on the seeming arbitrariness of the Spirit's
working. Those who are responsible for what
nowadays we call missionary strategy have
always the difficult task of keeping in touch with
the tides and currents of the Spirit of God as He
pursues His " immemorial plan."

Now this apparently fortuitous element in the
grand work of redemption, and which inci-
dentally can be seen on a small scale in the
working of any local church in which the Spirit
is operating at all, is singularly exasperating to
the tidy-minded. What God works in one place
or in one person, ought, we feel, to work in all
places and in all persons. But we are not dealing
with, shall we say, an electrical circuit in which
the power of electricity can always be relied upon
to do the same thing under the same conditions.
We are not using an impersonal force, and if
there is any question of using, it is He who uses
us and not we Him. God is of course really
moving, with what, from His point of view, if I
may say so reverently, I can only describe as

celestial ingenuity. But to us, who at the most only know the superficial facts of the situation, His actions may at times appear arbitrary or even capricious. I do not think we need to go "all solemn" about this, or to over-emphasise our own ignorance and sinfulness. It is surely far better to accept with good humour the situation as it is—that His thoughts are higher than our thoughts, and His ways higher than our ways (Isaiah lv. 8-9); and to realise that though we are called to this tremendous task of co-operation with Him, and are no longer servants but friends, we still need to be most humble, teachable and flexible as we follow His leading.

Another of our human weaknesses is to expect our own experience of God to be reproduced in identical terms in the experience of another. Worse than this, we sometimes tend to think that if another's experience is not the same as ours, it must be either spurious or incomplete. Now here we must be very firm with ourselves and use our common sense as well as our charity. People themselves differ greatly in their capacities and gifts, and also in their particular inward needs. One may need to be provoked and challenged by the Spirit of God, another may need relaxation and the release of laughter by the same Spirit. One may need painful lessons to reduce pride and over-confidence; another may need tender love and encouragement by the same Spirit. We all tend to overlook the beam in our own eye to which we are so accustomed, and to magnify the mote which is in our brother's eye. Only God knows the relative size and importance of the assorted beams and motes that exist between us, and much the most sensible thing to do is to leave God to deal with each individual Christian with the infinite variety and delicacy of His own love and wisdom. If we feel we must do something about the spiritual life of another Christian, the most constructive thing we can do is to keep our hands off and our tongues quiet, and to pray.

St. Paul is very rarely amusing, but the passage in 1 Corinthians xii about the various parts of the body is not without its humour. The idea of the human body being one huge ear, for example, or one vast eye, strikes me as not without humorous possibilities. And indeed the sense of humour, which is closely allied to the sense of proportion, is an essential part of the equipment of those who are called to work together in the service of God. The spirit which St. Paul illustrates in this passage is by no means dead. For example, in his enthusiasm the evangelist often finds it difficult seriously to imagine that anyone could be called *not* to be an evangelist. The man of vision and imagination finds it difficult to see the value of those who do no more than plod on faithfully along a well-tried road. The man whose concern is personal dealing with people and leading them to understand God better finds it difficult to be patient with the theologian or the Christian philosopher whose work is in the quiet of a book-lined study. Yet the truth is that the wholeness which God is working to achieve is never complete in an individual, but through individuals living together as one body, each supplying the deficiencies of the others. I hesitate to speak of that of which I know little, but surely this is true too of differing racial characteristics. The Englishman, the African, and the Indian, for example, may exhibit a certain limited wholeness in themselves and in their own church, but it is only when they learn to work together that they begin to realise a greater wholeness than they had previously imagined—the wholeness of the " one new man " in Christ.

This particular problem of wholeness may press upon the individual in different ways,

according to vision, temperament and spiritual
experience. What I am pleading for here is the
recognition that there are three fairly well defined
stages of the work of God in making men whole,
though, of course, they are all very much inter-
related.

The first is the stage at which a man sees himself, either instantaneously or gradually, as a
personality in conflict with itself. By contact
with the love of God, through which he is reconciled to His Father, he realises his true self. By
the power of God's Spirit within him, he is
able to stand and grow and work as a whole
man, though obviously at any given time he
is far from realising God's complete plan for
him.

Then, since Christians have need not only of
God but of each other, there is the stage where
a man realises his need of his fellow Christians
and their need of him. Again, the process may
be quick or slow, but sooner or later he realises
the truth of St. Paul's famous passage in 1 Corinthians xii, that there are " many members, yet
but one body " (v. 20, *A.V.*). He realises too
that " Men have different gifts, but it is the
same Spirit Who gives them " (v. 4), and that it
is only by true fellowship and co-operation with

others that any kind of wholeness can come into being in the local community.

The third stage, and here the best of us are but learners, is to realise not in theory but in practice that in this world that God has made, the various races, with their particular contributions, need one another to make the " one new man." There is no practicable way of achieving this except through the common realisation of sonship through Christ. All of us who have had any experience of Christian fellowship with other races know the thrilling and heart-warming sense of unity which we thus experience ; a unity which would not be possible except through a shared realisation of God through Christ. Some parts of the Church are plainly far in advance of others in experiencing this enriching wholeness, but all of us have a long way to go before we see how far-reaching the plan of wholeness really is. There is a good deal of prejudice, often unconscious, to be overcome, and a good deal of blindness to be illuminated ; sacrifices must be made and springs of charity unsealed, before this wholeness of mankind becomes a practical proposition. Yet there can be no doubt that it is towards this experience of wholeness that the Spirit of God is gently but remorselessly driving us all, and any step we take towards it is a step in the right direction.

These are the three stages normally experienced in comprehending the gist of the divine purpose. But there is a fourth stage, a fourth dimension, of which we have an inkling as soon as we embark upon "eternal life" in the here-and-now—the *fact* of what, for want of a better name, we call eternity. No follower of Christ goes on for long or far without realising both the utter necessity as well as the grandeur of this immense back-cloth against which our brief life is set.

Our forefathers of a few generations ago, though they made many grave mistakes and had several remarkable blind-spots, were for the most part conscious that they lived *sub specie æternitatis*. They may have had crude ideas about rewards and punishments, heaven and hell, but at least they believed that this life was to be lived responsibly with an eye to future destiny. Their idea of heaven may not commend itself to us, but they certainly believed that this transitory life was but a prelude to a sharing in the bliss of life hereafter. And from that belief they derived both comfort and courage.

To-day the picture is changed indeed. In a sharp reaction from the idea that " this little life can't matter very much anyway," and that " souls are more important than bodies," a vast amount of Christian thought and action is spent upon the improvement and development of man in this temporary set-up. No harm in that, surely, you may object. Of course not ; but if we swing too far we find ourselves party to a point of view which only tolerates Christianity because of its social implications ; because it tends to stabilise the home, to improve health and living conditions, or to reduce the rate of juvenile delinquency. Before we know where we are we have lost the authentic, other-worldly note ; we find ourselves regarding death, like any pagan, as an utter disaster ; and, like any disillusioned humanist, becoming bitterly disappointed that men do not always " love the highest when they see it." The emphasis, you see, even among Christians has shifted to this world, and to a large extent we have forgotten that " we have no permanent city here on earth, we are looking for one in the world to come " (Hebrews xiii. 14).

In the early Church the sense of eternity being only a hand's breadth off is very strong. This was

partly, of course, because its members momen-
tarily expected the personal return of Christ,
which would mean eternity breaking through into
this little sin-infected world ; partly because
death by martyrdom was never very far from
them or their friends, and this would mean not
disaster but being received into the presence of
Christ ; and partly, because of the overt and
obvious godlessness of the surrounding world
they laid up their " treasure in heaven " (St.
Matthew vi. 20), and reached out " for the
highest gifts of Heaven, where your Master
reigns in power " (Colossians iii. 2). It is true
that their Master had taught them to pray :
" May Your Kingdom come, and Your Will be
done on earth as it is in Heaven " (St. Matthew
vi. 10), and they lived that prayer as well as
prayed it. Yet they do not seem to have been
unduly worried that the Kingdom might be
barely established, the Will done by a mere
handful, before eternity, the Real Order, came
breaking through in power and vindication.

Plainly, as the hope of Christ's coming faded,
persecution ceased, and the Church grew rich,
powerful and influential, this sense of an im-
minent reality in which all Christians were rooted
began to lose its vividness and its urgency. Yet

the sense of eternity was never altogether lost, and it is not until we come to quite modern times that we find *among Christians* an insistence on the value of God's work in this world and a rather horrifying vagueness about the real world beyond.

Christians to-day are naturally revolted by the kind of Victorian piety which could exploit the physical energies of men, women and children and then spend a small part of the proceeds in building mission-halls to save their souls! No doubt unconsciously they are reacting sharply against that kind of attitude. Yet in their passionate affirmation of the relevance of the Christian faith to the whole needs of man, spiritual, mental and physical—and heaven knows it is the only faith which is really relevant to those needs—they sometimes lose sight of the transitory nature of this present life, and the glory and magnificence of the life to come.

I should like to hear St. Paul reply to the Communist gibe :

> Work all day, live on hay,
> There is pie in the sky
> When you die.

I am certain that to St. Paul and his contem-
poraries the quality of the pie in the sky is such
that it honestly does not matter if you do work
all day and live on hay on your way towards it !
" In my opinion whatever we may have to go
through now is less than nothing compared with
the magnificent future God has planned for us "
(Romans viii. 18). To him heaven was not some
shadowy compensation and reward but a solid
" weight of glory " (2 Corinthians iv. 17, *A.V.*),
no doubt indefinable in earthly terms, but none
the less permanent and utterly dependable. Such
a faith was certainly no " opiate of the people "
to these early Christians ; the certainty of being
sons of eternity gave them a fire and a cutting
edge which the Church has rarely equalled
since.

Again, lacking the background of eternity we
grow, if we are not careful, too high and mighty
to think of reward. We work for the good of
our fellows and we despise the " profit motive."
Yet Jesus Himself quite frequently spoke of
both rewards and punishments in the real world
and did not appear to despise consideration of
either. And while He exposed the folly of earthly
treasure-seeking, He strongly commended laying
up " treasure in heaven " (St. Matthew vi. 20),

and indicated the kind of conduct of which He could predict " your reward in heaven is magnificent" (St. Matthew v. 12). St. Paul, for all his tremendous sense of that real world to which he belonged, was not so superior that he could not write " wherefore we labour, that . . . we may be accepted of him.· (2 Corinthians v. 9, *A.V.*). Is it because we are affected far more than we know by the prevailing scepticism of our age about the world to come that we place nearly all our emphasis upon the present ?

It may well be asked what this consideration of eternity has to do with our present task of " making men whole " in the Name and power of Christ. Yet it is in fact most relevant, because without this dimension of eternity we doom ourselves to bitter disappointment and frustration, besides leaving ourselves with an altogether unmanageable burden of insoluble problems. Quite literally we take too much upon ourselves when we refuse to believe in " the ages to come " (Ephesians ii. 7, *A.V.*). With true poetic insight Browning wrote : " On earth the broken arcs ; in heaven, a perfect round." Unless we hold firmly to our rooting in eternity we shall be left with an awkward armful of broken arcs which

no ingenuity can assemble into a perfect round !
The fact is that eternity is an essential part of
man's existence as a son of God, and without it
there is no perfect wholeness. There is neither
time nor room enough in this cramped and limited
life for anything but the beginnings, decisive
and pregnant though they are, of Christ's tremendous work.

There is a certain pitiable absurdity about the
humanist who loves his fellow men but has no
belief in any life beyond the grave ; and this
may be a salutary object-lesson to Christians who
have nothing but the vaguest belief in the reality
that is to come.

Let us, the humanist says in effect, work for
the good of mankind, teaching, healing, improv-
ing. We shall always be " working for posterity,"
but that is a fine unselfish thing to do and we
must not mind that. Very well then, let us
assume that this fine work is successful and that
in the remote future the human beings then living
on this planet will have conquered Nature by
scientific knowledge. All tensions and malad-
justments of personality will have been removed
by vastly improved psychological methods, and
men and women will be unbelievably healthy,
wealthy and wise. But, what after that ? This

planet will eventually cease to be able to support life or will be destroyed by collision with another celestial body, This means that the sum total of human progress, of every effort and aspiration and ideal, will be annihilation in the deathly cold of inter-stellar space. *And there is nothing more to come.* Of course if men stop short of the final scene they may persuade themselves that the eventual happiness of our descendants a million years hence is a worthy ideal for which to live and die. But if the end of it all is *nothing, sheer non-existence*, surely no one but a fool can call that an ideal worthy of his adult allegiance.

But supposing this life is the preparatory school, the experimental stage, the probationary period, the mere prelude to real living on such a wide and magnificent scale that the imagination reels at the thought of it—then what exciting hopes invade our hearts! Indeed we already have inklings and intuitions that these things are true. " So long as we are clothed in this temporary dwelling we have a painful longing," wrote St. Paul (2 Corinthians v. 4) ; yet why in fact should we have this painful longing unless it is that we are born for a higher estate, destined for " that magnificent liberty which can only

belong to the children of God " (Romans viii.
21)? To change the metaphor, we are like
deep-sea divers moving slowly and clumsily in
the dim twilight of the depths and we have our
work to do. But this is not our element, and
the relief of the diver in coming back to fresh
air and sunlight and the sight of familiar faces is
but a poor picture of the unspeakable delight
with which we shall emerge from our necessary
imprisonment into the loveliness and satisfaction
of our true Home. It will be tears of joy as well
as of sorrow that God will wipe away from our
faces in that day (Revelation vii. 17).

It is against such a solid and reliable background
that we are called to live as strangers and
pilgrims in this evil and imperfect world. Our
certainty of that background must not of course
lead us to look upon this life as no more than a
tiresome interlude, and so to fix our minds upon
the heavenly vision that we fail to see and
respond to the needs all around us ! But I do
not seriously think there is much danger of that.
It is the man who is *not* certain of God, *not*
certain of the vastness of God's patience, and
not certain of the reality of eternity, who grows
cynical and loses hope. What after all can such
a man say to the one who is born blind and

deaf, to the mentally deficient, to the victim of incurable disease, to the parents of an only child killed in a tragic accident ?

How right was St. Paul when he wrote: " If our faith in Christ were limited to this life only, we should, of all mankind, be the most to be pitied " (1 Corinthians xv. 19). But our hope in Christ is not confined to this life ; we dare not limit His work to this little temporary stage. Behind all our strivings and our prayers there lies the unchanging purpose of God. Behind our imperfections lies His utter perfection. We see His work of " making men whole " begun, but we never see it complete. We see His Kingdom growing in size and strength, but we never see it universally established. Do we need to be reminded that as time goes on the numerical strength of that Kingdom in the unseen world outnumbers more and more the Church on earth ? His Kingdom, in truth, is not of this world.

We do not know the ultimate purpose of God ; the most we can do here is to see and to know " in part " (1 Corinthians xiii. 9, A.V.). But we can see the out-working in time and space of a vast plan whose roots are in eternity. It is something far greater, more far-reaching, more noble, more generous than most of our fore-

fathers could imagine. We cannot shut our eyes
to the breadth and depth of that purpose. The
highest, the best and the most satisfying thing
that we can do is to ask to be allowed to co-
operate with God's infinite patience in making
men whole.

THE END